SKIN RAFTS

SKIN RAFTS

KELWYN SOLE

S K I N   R A F T S

Publication © Hands-On Books 2022

Text © Kelwyn Sole
First published in Cape Town by Hands-On Books 2022
modjajibooks.co.za/genres/hands-on/

ISBN No. 978-1-928433-39-2

Design and typesetting by Stephen Symons
Cover design by Stephen Symons
Author photograph: Poetry Africa

Set in Sabon 9.5/14pt

A new stanza begins on a new page.

We are using our own skins for wallpaper and we cannot win.
     – John Berryman

you are not lost in the least,
but a deliberate deserter.
     – Ada Limón

My skin the wind, it's gone
kiting …
     – Vahni Capildeo

What can you do? We on earth
play at being people.
     – Gennady Aygi

CONTENTS

Prelude

Who will come with me through the fields
as they darken, by yourself, for yourself only,
the precise moment dusk clenches its fist
hard enough to bruise, pummel at your face?

Who'll be tempted enough to wish to vanish
from the yard where last night's braai still
smoulders (loading ash, parcel by parcel,
into the immense moving trucks of the wind)

and, tossing that cigarette half-smoked away
as if nonchalantly, start to cough, be mortified,
deny all the trite words that have come to life
day by day, one by one, out of your mouth?

… If you want to baffle the insect of time
that tickles on everyone's wrist and lulls
till it stings, it's time to come out …

                              trample
your garden with its goal of mere beauty;
burst through its hedges hemming you in
with sham protection, brittled by drought.

Don't you notice the future that's coiling up
and hissing to strike at your house?

Your walls bubble under a patina of old paint
and the slaver of many too many sad winters;
your curtains still shut tight for no earthly reason;
till all you own reeks of despair and decay:

tonight your face looms, a ghost on its pillow,
tears trickle down on the linen you've convulsed,

you're never at peace with your dreams in affray
and I know I can't help you. I need to find out

who you are, who I am – we grow old in this place!
No one was born for this, here no one can smile:

you are my neighbour: surely you know?

Just up the road

Young men with neatly trimmed beards and weary eyes
gaze meditatively into the maws of silver oysters
                    seeking pearls of data,
                        treasure troves of information,

in the free wifi café on the corner
where suburbia meets the world
                            only
fleetingly.

            Their fingers nibble at the real –

across the floor a mouse, unseen, skitters:
nudges briefly in the gloom at the crumblings
of energy bars and splatterings of coffee
which allow them all to keep wobbling
upon their tightropes of the gig economy.

It goes on to sniff at their sandalled toes,
inquisitively ...

                outside, a stone's throw away,
salivating with a longing which will not
outlive his own decrepitude, a beggar hungers.

Alone within him, lurks
                    what's left
of the crackle of the self:
an outmoded radio.

Landscoping

Soft watches for a Peninsula

The sleepwrecked day stretches,
waves barter foam with the sky;
the hours begin to roll, divide work
away from that tangent on which
those jobless do not ride but flail,
fade into the distance away from
our trains of thought
                      faces
sound their tocsins of weariness,
the nose of sleep wrinkled by
paraffin breathes in: a single
cellphone tower leaves its shadow
groping across a land of drought,
wooden shacks and scoured roofs

transfixed by a maritime wind
with no glimpse of the ocean
blue lights of police vans pass

crows take off into the wind

once more, my people do not use
this dawn for their awakening

     *   *   *

There's light –
somewhere a sun must be floating up
on a cushion of lustrous mist ...
nacreous,
almost luminescent,
a screech of rays starting
to break through –

a humming-bird moth a stipple
of gold
          probing with
an invisibly thin tongue
into the flowers'
maddened cerise

*   *   *

A white bakkie flashes in and out
of existence on the road as it
passes under the dark parenthesis
of tree after tree after tree: above
only the shrike flies, watching
with its pauper's eye – like ours,
a fierce compulsion of hunger

*   *   *

As the sun's shafts march
one by one across
the rise and fall of sand
to ambush what's left
of darkness
within a shack
propped up among the dunes

an old woman shitting
on a long drop
eats an apple, chews
at love, her memory of it,
then slowly swallows –

but spits out every pip

*   *   *

Spent emotions wobble away from each other

like those cartons of eggs – just over there! –
forgotten on the roof of a taxi that takes off
from the spaza shop
at speed
       but not falling, not yet

*   *   *

The peeling skin of a path
between Station A and Station B
through a wilderland of scrub
pricked by blackjacks and rusty cans
takes one to the secret cemetery

known only to the serial killer
and the bones of the women
he has dismembered there

*   *   *

For a moment the air
in imagination
stills, coagulates,
                    seems to
arrange the landscape into
mere surface
                    becomes a painting

until the wind again antiquates
to craquelure

                    whatever truth
you thought was framed
right there in front of you

and it all blows away –

so the pee of a little boy,
suspended unnaturally in mid-air,
splashes anew into
a tinkling hosanna
                    the dog
stuck seemingly as afterthought
in the left lower corner begins again
to gambol with its ball and farts, loudly,
without warning
                    or remonstrance
from the little girl whose pet it is

who, in turn, stubs her toe on something
no little girl nor boy ever saw before
in art, and cries, grasping
that none of them have

any knowledge of perspective

*   *   *

It is strange to hear the toads
gone from their wordings
where they wandered through
gardens seeking a purer water,

from the springs
they had abandoned to faeces
and plastic and the duped
thirst of bloating cows

… the sea's backwash rusts with sewage:
waves break yellow, the colour of bone
as the sea yawns, and yawns again,
disclosing oblivious surfers
who wobble on
their toothpicks
           in its rotten teeth

*   *   *

Over the balcony
of the boutique
hotel between an
Australian flag
and a French
flag hanging
in welcome
above the street
it is possible to
look down, watch
the detritus of
commerce and
history, their
small figures,
one by one
stumble and go
in and out in
and out of
the *drankwinkel*
across the way

*   *   *

Leading off the corridors back of
the travel lodge: a spa. Occasionally

women in brown housegowns,
towels swirled round their hair

pad from one room to the next,
like sauntering ice cream cones

*   *   *

Lured by so many flypapers
of beauty
           tourists' voices buzz

their faces shimmer
lifted up to the Mountain
with an awe that blinds them
to who we really are
who live here
               in all
the places they're not looking:

our cars continue
to bluster, yowl for further speed
along potholed highways, while money
learns new ways to rap
and street-talk

though our integuments of skin
never bring us to an insight of ourselves
outside the age-old definitions
year in, year out …

*   *   *

In the heat
the summer is a vein
throbbing with life

a hummed undertone of
chops pap and wors
strikes discordant notes
across the lawn

sanguine hymns from
the churches: a grumble
of drums insistent
from the mountains

two children in
a small backyard
test out swearwords
on each other.

In a harshening breeze
and oblique sunlight
the vlei beloved
by romantics
hints at what it holds:

mud stirred to the surface
becomes the colour
of a drying scab

*   *   *

Nothing that illumines
comes from their sky,
though the sun beats
down. Squatting in
shade, in slivers
of memory

        old men
on benches debate
their bodies' inept
tinkering with the
years

*   *   *

A knife coated with rust or blood –
summarising someone's life –
lies hidden in the grass

*   *   *

Beaches measure out the hours
in decreasing glissandos of light:

filaments of sun tear at wisps of cloud
– fishhooks set to lose their fish –

pick fillets out of the afternoon's
flesh
      as it glimmers, then dims,
        to slide slowly
back into the sea

*   *   *

A sudden chill; the bloodstream
no longer sings, and Aldebaran
                    in the East
rising earlier and earlier
is not a human red –

*   *   *

Both horns of the waxing moon prod
the constellations across the heavens.
Akilter from the blue eyes of the Pleiades,
belt cinched into studs of ancient light,
Orion reels his mad, measured twirling
dance through the night. What quarry
he endlessly pursues, who can tell?

Two oceans: the foreboding

Days like sheep herded
across a field: bleating
days, no longer ordained
by any shepherd's crook
of meaning

        where do we go,
when the words we choose
to live by are all we can see?

– when all around us
Cape Town flares
its whiskers, hides
its rats' nests
of empty hearts
and broken homes
in the dazzle of the bay
and, under its blue blanket,
the cold knees of the Atlantic
begin to stir, then
kick out?

        A long nerve of clouds
amasses on
the horizon.
        Deep uneasiness
stirs through our bones

though we decide
we cannot move:

just await (again)
a coming storm.

Two océans: the yearning

Flayed by cold, evening
forces me inside
            away from the Scorpion
upthrusting; and the lights of the harbour
in the distance blear as I close windows
fudged by crystals of salt
                   until I can
no longer see
no longer know

            that vast domain,
            its rise and fall
under my feet

inescapable
movement beneath

tugged by the moon
               into rhythms
of possibility   inscrutable gift

awash

with life lessons
            in how to brace steady.

Though it is perilous
to hear the sea sirening
if you cannot swim

I wish my life were out
there once more, bobbing
on its raft of skin.

Surfers

Over and over the surfers
enter the surf, but these days
just one side of the beach – raise
middle fingers at the suppers, try
to make them enter on the other

as far away as possible… .

Glared at by both sides, by
enforcers of the rival codes,
a girl supper and boy
surfer share a spliff,
reclining on a dune

still hot with what sand's not
yet been attended to by dogs.

Backwards, forwards, to and
fro they inhale, then exhale,
grunting with satisfaction;
to them it doesn't matter
if their peer groups peer,

or grumble about 'wave etiquette' –
or demand a ban on hydrofoils –
or curse each others' false *sang froid* –.

Their wetsuits glisten with
shucked water as if they
had just emerged from
their mothers' wombs,
neophytes neopreening,

throbbing with discovery
of lust,
        they're explorers;
a new Romeo and Juliet
setting out in earnest

to map the riptides of flesh
(and be dumped in its backwash).

*   *   *

An aging surfer
lifts one foot,
then another,
as exercise:
then one leg
high, higher,
then the other …

becomes
an ungainly crane

about to re-enter
its native sea
with some assurance:

… or something else …

                    a creature
from the black lagoon?

*   *   *

Meditating in a wet suit
a young woman in the lotus position
contemplates
        with serenity
the nurdle-laden sea.

Farm

The Robin by the drainage line's
more timid than is usual:
its wisping song dissembles,
scuttles unseen through tangles
of desiccated grass and under aloes
till we're hoodwinked
                              but the Chats
make up for it. Appearing
one by one through a chink
in a barn's rotting wall, they
swivel heads – always so careful
of the world – then transform to a
sudden swift succession; flick
wings, one by one, once settled on
a strand of wire. There's a growing
line of them – eight, nine. Ten.

Oatmeal bubbles: a whiff
of dagga. Don't worry. Your
ersatz hunger will be seasoned,
palpably, with salt and butter.

The empty stomach of the earth
feeding through its creatures slowly
appears despite a stubborn mist,
sinks into your own to settle
there, and stick. But the farm
is of little use these days:
sows its own image onto websites
to supplicate a stream of tourists

… there is no heft left in my arm, to test
the blunt axe rusting on its stump.

Under the rafters spiders have
hung out their transparent washing.

   2

Grudging heat claims us
not. Though a crippled sun awakens,
leans falteringly against the day

it's hard to know this morning why
 – not how – its meagre light can be seen
above the mountains; because
the slow, trembling diffusion down
is just a tentative *hello*, a beginning
to a sentence that none of us
imagine can ever be completed

and I can no longer credit here what
belief is mine. Immensities of cloud
don't dilute dread: I sit beneath
these bartered, timeshared eaves
where biltong swings, bracketed
by marbles of fat,
                    dangles
and flirts with its suitor flies

or, turning the other way, find
the land undulating away to bring
to sight as evidence
                         copses, cows,
but also the makeshift houses where
poverty is shy enough to seem
almost to shrug itself into acceptance.

  3

As I stroll past his stoep, the farmer
pops his head around a corner

gestures me towards a chair
not too far from derelict

... *Come and sit, though I don't*
know where my children are

who have, I think, heard
too much already:

grown ugly to themselves
because of the contempt

that limns
the eyes of others –

on every farm across this valley
life is not so much pressed down
by gravity as the weight of a history
no one can escape

                  glued by intentions,
good mixed mainly with malign –
a yearning for land which has always
required deaths and dispossession
and still does, for completion;
in such a way that no future no
further can be descried
but wounded

          oh

             my ears are filthy
with the platitudes smeared into them
as the world cracks from drought
and the trust of young children bleeds
its oil beside the scatterings of stolen
sunflower seeds they were roasting
until the farmer found their hunger,
and sjambokked them
to order

          and their fathers' and their
grandfathers' ghosts tick, timed bombs
within their graves, remembering
the robbing of pastures, their house
walls bulldozed, toppling,

                while the farmer
in his turn cannot forget the intruders
in his house:

          how, after her beating,
the tortured fingertips' blood
his daughter spilled made bright
patterns on their worn rug …

and his fury mounts – as did theirs –
in the telling, and retelling.

The 'land question.' Black, white,
flung apart on a centrifuge of need
with our futures scattered ripening
for murder. The devil is a skin
our own we wrap so tightly round
all the places we can look out from
until we see no more, any longer
                                    just
a symbolic expanse of grief and memory
stretching towards each possible horizon,
fertilized forever with the dung of anger.

4

As for now, who can fill mouths
with something more tangible
than promises?
                    My wife,
he says, *always wanted to grow*
unusual things, have beautiful things
around her: but there was frost,
then drought: so in this, the second
decade of her passing, her peach trees
no longer bear fruit, nor blossom….

I smile at him, inhale the steam,
the vapour of his *boeretroos*.
But a sentence whispers
at my mind - dare I say it? –
that

    nothing has ever happened here
without the labour of the landless -
and

    nothing will happen here again
if you do not open up these fields
to the labour of the landless …

but no. My need for words

evaporates, vanished
with any other word to share
that could begin to heal –

as far as I can see in all directions

every compass point remains misted,
or invisible.

       … I think I'll sit here
until I am convinced enough
that my silence bleeds.

Our endless dying

Another funeral, in which
one side or the other celebrates
its impending decomposition.

Do we always have to live by bad example?
– after having carefully scrubbed away
all semblance that it was
to truth.

> Always, the burning tyre,
> > the rubber bullet.

Our accounts of this gyre and twist
into fantastical shapes

– the hero, the villain –

but in the end
it's only the victim will keep still.

Whiteness for the prosecution

Whiteness
can remember a time when things were not as they are now.

Whiteness
can sense the tsk-tsk of history murmuring in its blood, wagging a
warning.

Whiteness
finds no redeeming myth to be deceived by more epic than stocks and shares.

Whiteness
is not a colour but a powder that flakes off of Rand notes which (when
rubbed between the fingers) starts to stain the soul.

Whiteness
gets so bored it sits in the home or workplace refusing to go outside, all the
while shooting the breeze with White Monotony Capital.

Whiteness
breeds nonchalance: unaware that, if its thoughts deviate in new directions,
they're likely to be autocorrected by the machineries of privilege.

Whiteness
wants to learn about its other countrymen and -women only when feeling
threatened enough by them to do so.

Whiteness
prefers to view Africa as a symbol, getting confused by the bipolarity
of its details.

Whiteness
often tends – even when it's teasing – to end up in the missionary position.

Whiteness
doesn't take its clothes off before others say it's cool.

Whiteness
is very surprised when its good intentions are told to fuck off.

Whiteness
thinks it's still just to give alms to a beggar's legacy.

Whiteness
can be so repentantly apologetic that its spine gives up on it and goes to live with someone else.

Whiteness
will never know whether to reach for the braai grill or the gun.

Whiteness
has learned how and when to keep its head down.

The 'white left'

Don't tell them it was guesswork:
that we were abstracted from the start,
children who'd played on manicured
squares of lawn with servants poised
at the edge of their vision, secateurs
ready to do the adults' every bidding,
who – because we were children –
could pick up the unspoken miasma
of anger more swiftly than our parents.

Don't tell them that we, grown painfully
up, spoke to the common man in riddles,
expected rain from the dry seasons' sky;
that we persevered past the end of kindness,
judged our friends as much as our enemies,
kept watching dust motes whirl around that
single tree striving to fruit within the yard
of the suburban commune our so temporary
home
        from which we ventured, given time,
to find the Other, a place of refuge
from ourselves to which we thought we
could be faithful. But then, of course,
we heard the screams that followed,
and only the bravest could persist,
those with enough bluster in them
to tone down all the doubts muttering
within
        and join a different kind of Party,
ululating from apprenticed tonsils:
part of a melting pot that was destined
over time to falter and then melt … .

For now we know the soul rips apart
under siege, tips under from the continued
squalor of watching brutality and squalor
that's still set unabashed all around us.
We've grown old on inherited stoeps,
gazing out over stubborn landscapes
of beauty made toxic by the histories
they've enacted, and keep on enacting.
It's impossible to get rid of the past:
to dig the bodies up, the limbs sundered
by cruelty and by grief; to reconstitute
ashes lost into wind, urns in cupboards,
the memories we're now forced to share
with monuments and suited dignitaries.

Does one calibrate between governments,
trust corrupt rulers who've supplanted
those much worse? Should anyone rejoice?
There is no way to find what's stored in us
so violent and so damaged; to recognise
we have only got more tired, cicatriced
by wariness and age, feet uncertain on
the good earth we helped fight for: yet
still stranded on four centuries of landfall
– and still, too often, just left white.

The empty space we call Mandela

On the Waterfront
four statues of Nobel Laureates
stand in a line, a platoon:
their proportions slightly wrong, they
seem not quite human, unsettling
the eye of everyone
                              not tourists.

Above wavecrests, in freshening
spray and wind, if you turn
the other way
                    Robben Island still
winks like a blinded eye in the socket
of the Bay.

              Disembodied not by death,
but long before: dismayed, dismaying,
floating above our moral carnage:
a name everyone invokes,
a stance no one can credit.

The empty space called Mandela.
Our empty spaces call Mandela.

In London a poet launches
his self-promoting barque of ignorance
with incantations to your legacy;
in Durban a performing Fallist
castigating the privileges
of everyone except
her own
                shits on your name,
in a different kind of posturing.

In a sense, I suppose, it was your fault:
Who were you, Mandela?

Impunity's the icon, these days,
that hides behind our icons

your Party's become a bacillus
that sickens everyone it touches.

In the cities, among the bustle
of commerce and bargained gossip,
the buildings are a sad ear longing
for your name.

                Could you ever,
can you tell us now just what to do,
now the resentments of race
spittle the lips of everyone,
now hatred scabs on every skin?

Streams flow past mile on mile of shacks
bearing poison from the mines, leaked sewage,
children playing in rubbish piles of diversity,
a rainbow nation of spilled oil –

our dreams dribbling out to sea with them

and all we find
are tongues that lick round every hunger,
creating new ones to be unhinged by

all we hear
are politicians whiffling, and the only
cheap things are their shots
                        though every one
still knows how to find the time
to mandela their features into a smile

all we see
are prophets preaching charms
                    to the colour of their skin,
who search for empty vessels
                    to dump their bile inside

a land divided –
a race right to the finish –

each night for hours your lamp
quails at all our windows, too meagre
too confusing to resolve
into new morning.

                Were you ever here,
Mandela?

Comprador

*...they show a certain anxiety to hide their real
convictions, to side track, and in short to set
themselves up as a popular force.*
                    - Frantz Fanon

Yo! Comprador!
                Here we are, years after liberation,
yet the poor man still stands at the side of the road
shouting into his cellphone as it loses charge,
the teenager who locked herself in an outside toilet
can't stop weeping, because her uncle is still roaming
free, his belt undone
                        and the families of child victims
refuse to be comforted, with their cases postponed again
or dockets vanished, or witnesses paid off:

so,
        as the sorrows and calamities pile up,
                                        I find it
fruitless to be a guest in the house of your betrayal,
impossible

            until you explain
                            what happened to our hopes
you raised then crushed, the many lives your greed's now
sullied? Look at you, lounging at ease, surrounded by
African masks, smart televisions, a picture of that leader
you in private vilify but in public praise. It's all a game
of weighted dice to you, a pack of cards you deal to hide
the sleight-of-hand
                        or any notion that the vanished kings
and queens you resurrect in fantasy had subjects: instead,
we must bear your endless games of racecardsharping

while you labour
                    to recruit their offspring to your version
of their history of pain, the black skins scourged for centuries,
that past from which you derive your interest,
the trauma where you invest your stock … .

Your passage down the years befuddles me:
warriors who waved slogans for freedom
and still call each other '*comrade*'
                              graduate over time
to faceless figures slouched expectantly in boardrooms
with the appeals to '*our people*' now fake news,
though you go on trying to guard those
frontiers of race with the nervous
diligence of landowners.

                    Too much of you
remains theatre: how many steps away from you
must we race to find a perspective that is truer,
to decode what's real in such orotundity?

The corporations wait patiently to claim you for themselves –
just how long's that leash that ties you to their kennels
of voracity,
                    that forces you to chase your own tails
on these whirligigs of uselessness?

Body language

40 shacks were destroyed in the blaze

1

You sifted the earth
from my body,
                hung
words on the doorframes
of my eyes:
                the elbows
of my sight dislocated

one singed sleeve
fluttering
                in the breeze
you thought
was a flag of hope

grain by grain
you owned my earth

my wife
skulls in her womb
she had not foreseen,
giving birth,
were there:

arms a-dangle
she stands in an alley
between two shacks
watching, smelling

firemen
and scorched human
                    meat -
a stench of loud voices
consoling her

the braille of blisters
on her fingertips touched
by her neighbours

my children
      a memory
soughing through
            zinc
            exploded glass

   2

What are you doing, with
my words?

            your renderings
that think they're gentle
                        tears

so you think you speak
on my behalf

dissolve away

the stone of
my reality,
my tiny reality:

my will a pebble heavy
in my gut, knocking beneath
my ribs
      a life that cannot
struggle out

my children dead
in their mother's arms
my family a map of blood
still has to hear

your words your
enormous words

I can sense them,
black or white,
in black and white,
their upstrokes suave
but incomplete
        as a judas kiss,
each one preparing
          for the down
stroke of its false regard

to complete my sentencing.

Kind

And always: *what kind are you?*
Following this: *Are you of our kind?*
I can only reply ... *well, kind of...*
and *that* only after mulling it over,
while you think that I seem to be
thinking too long. So, dialogue stops:
you shrug, start to look elsewhere:
But then, it takes all kinds, I suppose?
But I'm nothing of your kind, or what
you want to find: nation-tribe-race,
the borders you want to judge me by
so you can either choose to drop kind
words or not
                    or try to find
furious words to pay me back in kind.

Though – who knows? – I might not
be one wishing *to crawl with their kind*:
not one turning out a kind of a likeness
of the hatreds that dismember everything
we choose to remember. Then maybe I am
merely one of that kind who starts to
realise you're talking a kind of bullshit?
Whatsoever the case, it's time
to be honest:
                    my kind is just kind.

Facebook (with timeline)

1

A face   yes   but

my country has a broken sky
though this is not yet noticed

blue stretches to every horizon
while clouds, rain, stars in their processions
make us drowse through life
but my gaze is simple, too simple
to credit why so many dogs
pacing around each other
in this enclosed space
can whine and bark at the same time

still fed like slaves can be angry
at being called the same

what is lost

we had hoped to be   a thing

     of unnameable beauty.

2

Every day now I watch

storms' dark cloud-caterpillars
inch closer across the coastline
slowly nibble up the sun
yet somewhere in the nonsense
of my head remains a dream of
lightness. As if the earth

did not fill up with concrete
and plastic and the persistent
nightmares of thwarted profit;

as if each person's life did
not have to drag itself hand
over hand across a landfill of

broken promises and dreams.

We all move in parallel, alone,
through a world where self-love's poor
substitute for knowledge, and vaunting
tongues can never find community, despite what
the purveyors of their own faces think:
instead, a triggering of insults,
a parade of needs in violence –

the small steps of doves brinking a ledge.

My world's made stark by your choices,
mirror-men

3

        and your beliefs are not an option
if they do not help erase the blood and fear
ambushing our steps from living,
breath to breath;
           if we remain content
to become encased in fables of glory
of wounding and redemption
over and over again;
at what cost

       emerging
from the pedantry of the national earth,
ejecting a spit of clichés like
a cornered cobra?

Pity the victims and the victors
swapping faces throughout history,
who believe their axe swung towards
the Other's head can ever be a final blow … .

4

These days the people who pass by ask:
what is your name? And I answer:
I will trust you only if you
have forgotten yours.

I say to my name: leave me!
Let the dust of my journey
obscure what I have become,
the huff of my footsteps through
this desert of sand called meaning

but I also say: I want to find
those words that can be lived in before
they lose me again

even if I, like you, have come to forget
that the rocks and soil beneath us
have been secured with a foundation

of lies and rubbish.

From where can the self arise
in landscapes sated with
the empty stomachs of our history?

So here I am: forever nobody. Yet
as you swagger past me
profile after profile

remember

I've recorded all your names, though
you never can remember mine:

and that's the reason why
I am going to outlast you.

What needs to be said

I don't belong in demographics.

- Phillippa Yaa de Villiers

1

Many years ago two entered a home
but at this precise moment only one
of us can be asleep.

The grizzle of curls on your forehead
licks the sky. Is licked in turn with light,
    flecks of heaven.
    The trade of love
small gestures, to barter every day:

you on the couch, breathing
slow

your dancer's toes upturned   skewed
bent towards the sun.

2

To know a wife who hums to herself
around the house, tiring as days can be,
and gazes with equanimity on tea cups
or the raging ocean in the distance
that smashes
    its plates together
       and only says:
it's your turn to wash the dishes!

3

Words are just skin;
the body is the belovèd.

4

                              I open
my paper to the screech of race, I
open my inbox to the screech of race,
momentary faces of those apostles
of their own skins who caper
across the screen, self
important keyboard
mice
       then turn - is it fatigue
       at their choir of sameness? -
and see
         you, the love of my life –
our skins we give weight
though never final weight to
sublimated in a trust of thirty years,
a trust not built on colour.

As the adventure
of old age begins and we raft towards
quieter waters, your hand always
calming as a kiss reaches out
to mine
       the lines of head and heart along
your palm creased into wisdom: you,
traveller, dancer across time's seasons, your
life that gives its generosity to the world:
the slow murmur of your heart engaged
as usual, whatever you may be doing ...

and mine, blessed because beside yours.

For love

If there's always a slow blues
to breathe out about my life

it's sharded, splintered through
surprising interruptions by love

– as she stood there, once,
wrapped up against the winter

by a promise of her nakedness
in spring. So every dawn remains

our one our only true iconoclast,
breaking cliché down into possibility.

The feel of her: her lines of speech,
a lure of the slight tension and flex

of her earthly weight slightly athwart
any pull of gravity, that leads on

– at an obverse angle – into surprise.
We, twins in laughter conjoined

by an embrace, by what we stumble
towards; with eyes on the jugular

of fulfilment, a hint of happiness,
an itch of joy under each skin

that cannot be scratched away.
Nothing sad alights where

our fingers are. We never can
be lost this way. Our names.

People in glass houses

1

And what if her glass house is full of birds?

From outside he sees only its windows,
reflections that peck at a bread of clouds
where nothing chirps, nothing
tells him anything of
                                        her

and she

looking out, finds no proportion: the relation
of horizon to next horizon baffles sight …
be it to the mountains, sky, or
– as she squints – even to the space
between her eyes and lashes.

Neither of them gazes out, or in,
in any way that mollifies perspective,
or lets it settle in their grip.

2

Each night

the silhouette of his writing hand
holding the memory of the woman
it once caressed shadows his book,
lifts the words he once said to her
from their paper graveyard

again they are alive, in flight;
flutter towards the mirrors
in which she lives,

that somewhere she sleeps among her vistas.

… It's cold, outside.
The world is quiet
                    moonless
he can see through
no glass darkly;
though

above them both
light gapes its beak
from the nest of every star.

3

How far, or close, their places of desire.

New lovers

Though this joining of hands has been done
before, by other couples much like them

their trepidation teems, nests its swarm
of wasps in the cracked bole of the heart –

the uncanny, she says, *makes me shudder,*
but it's like what's left of the solar wind:

you can only sense it if you start to sweat
at night, in cold like this, believing heat
can reach out at you through the void....

Now here it is, trapped inside his body.

The adjoining beach is calamitous with sound
through louring weather. In a lea
they're behind dunes so darkened
they may as well be forested
so deep they are in
a garden of shadows
                        that only
storm-moan through whipping marram
shoots from the moon whatever bullets
of light can still wound either's face
                                        where
they recline,
            facing each other,
                                stretched out:

her teeth shimmering as she mouthes

I recognised you from the first ….

After that, there in no way for him to
think how to break this stillness. Perhaps
they must avoid the curse of light
forever. Stay washed in shadow

or merge, to shake off the inner darknesses
that hound them; find a way to look out
much as a squirrel enjoys the sunshine:
with one eye cocked, and carefully.

Though none of this will last, eternity
has no word to utter who they are:
and death is just a place where love
speaks still, despite their silence.

Even the sea, for all its immensities,
cannot reach as far as the huge space
spanned when their fingers, extending,
touch.

They are at rest, and calmed.

Lacking the horse

Waves kill themselves in serried rows.
The beach is sucked away is piled up,
the shoreline shifts –

constantly the sea destroys its silence.
Its concealments are vomited on the beach,
the contents of a stomach

offered up in front of us: fetid ribbons
of fat kelp that lollop on the hoofmarks
slowly filling up

of a distant horse.
Your peasant's feet,
toes with their broad and rippled nails
dig into wet sand –

backwash exposes them you brace yourself
but slip
       and once more each toe founders,
starts to drown.

I brush the soft, goosebumped flesh
above the collarbone – your collarbone –
with a finger

and we forget about
finding the horse.

Orature

your gasping for breath

> the granulated nub of your pleasure
> rubbed across my tongue

my gasping for breath

> the warm shock
> of your mouth around me

no one can write this

Five befuddled moons

1

Space and the passing of full moon
in front of my eyes;

night stridulates with nude insects,
can't discover silence

sirens flicker in their panic near
by, but for now

I am once more a man of sorrow,
elbows on knees

palm indenting cheek, a dissonance
uttered into flesh.

Among the ruins of my music,
my voice …

the language given me no longer
sings: swings

between stuttering and bluster.
But I must

believe the world can breathe. A hint
of fog hazes

the horizon, then moves its filched
chiffon away

– a faint urge to thunder somewhere,
never true to rain –

this is a time when the human spirit
pickpockets all

it can see or hear, for what it needs to
find as meaning.

   2

Tonight it's about the codling-moth moon
that has not appeared as it should
over the squalling branches of these dark thickets
but eaten slightly out of shape: a shaky pendant
on the tree of constellations, a child's toy,
a punctured balloon of wan light.

   3

Moon's now
         in decline:
her radiance has gone arthritic
and her reflection hobbles
gamely between walls,
along locked gates
parked cars
        but stops
     to commiserate
with every face –

4

Honed
sharp, a blood moon looms,
bent coin
              aloft, awkward
in its slow skitter
across heaven

                briefly
makes night
burnish to a pewter

balks,

and still will not bare
our features
                crippled

by shadows.

5

Gripping the edge
of the coverlet

your face lingers
on a vestige of night:
so much stillness
around us

even the sound
of your breath
seems to hang
above the bed,
separate from me –

only one pale shaft
of derelict light
where the curtain
(blown open)
does not come
back to rest

reveals your face:
shows the tips
of two fingers
and a knuckle
of the other hand
whitened into bone.

What have we
become, moon-
struck?
        One shard
of light may be
enough to guide
our dreaming,

permit these open
snoring mouths
to know, at last,
a taste of calm

after love's
frenzied lunacy.

The beekeeper's husband

If her words could only buzz in the hive of his mind
like bees, tiny alchemists perpetually at work
to transmute what she feels into the slow magic
of honey
       if only
           her words to him could be
come swift, winging through a garden
                    that flares
its colours to his senses
           could float above grass, ride
any breeze, dodge between branches in a blurring of wings,
veer with
       the inspirations and aspirations of her breath
so that
      even as he waits, a bedraggled drone,
he could at least know the measure of her flight,
savour her speech, map the inclinations she has found
to steer between their home, the flowers and the sun;
her way of speaking beauty
          and may he then be
surprised by a returning sweetness, brought back to him
      despite the stings jabbed
under his skin
      ever harder to scrape away

      so that he too, amid
     the remorseless hum of the world
   could learn the figures of her dance,
awaken every morning
     to taste love in its making.

My country

I don't much value the confessional:
could tell you a few stories, sitting here,
but the clink of tin as my garden's can
of suet swings, marauded by squirrels,
confounds me
              until I hazard to point
out only what you've not noticed but
envelops us: of the birds now bereft
of their suet, calling in distress; of flies
wringing their hands for mercy; of slug
and snail journeys, seldom finished; of
fearful lizards never at ease, frantic
for a sudden hiding place to gape
ensorcelled into stone;
                      of ancient
rotting trees, so knotted they no longer
can find ways to ingratiate themselves
with any soil's embrace or gale's bluster.
I want to speak of the ugly creatures –
their recurring droughts of fulfilment as
they circle, and wish to worry to the final
bone, the carcase of their grievances.

… When may insight nimble up to us
delicate as a spider's tensile weaving
yet strong enough to keep the touch
between us, if only for a moment?
– a speaking out that's undistracted,
a labour truespun from the belly,
part of an earth that's fruiting –

                        I want to be
a citizen of
that country

            not retreat indoors each dusk
to counterfeits of light in dimmed rooms
where I fake comfort by rifling the pockets
of the dead for their words, yet end up
            always finding
            my vigil ends

            with the dogma
            of those tongues
which promise just a swarming
back   to root out more myths
and feast on them, the carrion
            of our history.

Woodpecker

Woodpecker in the forest's vast closed cupboard
raps to get out. But it can't. And the hammering
caroms from bill to bole, from tree to tree,
from ear to echo back to ear, till you are wholly
trapped within the collateral declensions of its hunger.
Nothing remains to twin any beat with its original –
just a kaleidophone of multiplying woodpeckers
afflicting wood with drumtaps whose single author's
lost. You can no longer tell the woodpecker for
the trees of sound: so here you stand, abashed,
hoping to conjure a path out of all the ricocheting
directions made possible around you, then recollect
exactly when your body began to shatter; to collect
the slivers of yourself which are now mere detritus
of the act – irretrievable – of a single thoughtless bird.

Birding

I asked directions from a passing bird

    I mistook for myself

and, though it swerved aside from my body,

    it answered me:

who knows, fool, what whims ossify at the wish

    bone of the unwinged?

Go find your own way to your catastrophes:

    till then perch, wait

        *   *   *

to be lifted up. The wind is opening its book,

    but you can't read

those words as wings printed upon its pages.

    Your sky is broken,

your passage always less than the distance

    you have to journey;

and I know your wisdom comes as fleetingly,

comes like birds

that congregate, hover, then disperse. Always

your song's in tatters:

for everything of yours wants to stand still.

Benign serpents

i. Eggeater

In the disguise of a Night Adder
(well, almost) this clown,
in a grotesquery of rage,

gapes its mouth
rasssps scales across each
other
      strikes out

– then isn't sure what to do next.

ii. Slugeater

Tabakrolletjie – little hero! –
conqueror of the magical spiral of galaxies
in its most tangible form:
the fortress of the snail.

iii. House Snake

A torpid snake
elegant and helpless
as an angel
         cannot flee the edge
         of your shovel's ignorance.

Breathless creatures

1. *Wooden Gull*

Sunlight lances through
the window
each afternoon as
our book pages turn
without fuss I wonder

do we keep time with the tides?
It's almost spacious enough
for the two of us, this hotel
room above a harbour ...

in the glassed-out distance
fishing boats
go in, go out

while a wooden seagull
painted the correct colours
carved ready for take off
sits wobbling on our table edge
between the shells, notepads
and complimentary wine.

A fly perched on its beak
mocks its lack of flight.

2. *Wire Shark*

Entanglements define it:
tensed around a spine wound
by a gnarled village hand

anxious for money
who cajoled it into
its unique shark shape.

Every day it swims
across an infinity of tiles:
not every being's
as brave through boredom.

Oh that jewelled blue eye!

I would like to set it free,
see what it does:

watch it plunge
                        into
the waves of conjecture.

3. *Birdbath*

Stone bowl-bearing
                              frog
attracting life: the glaucous eyes
stare away from the garden up
at the mountain
                              now only just visible
between burgeonings
                              of vibracrete
and glass seeded by the rich,
massive and infertile.

Canted against a slope
it tilts over, imperceptibly,
slops more water
every day.

It won't outlast this winter.

Wing. Water. Tree.

During the endlessly
black night
                invisible owls
duet above a spreading
rash of city lights,
once their sovereign
hunting grounds

then take off
so silently

only the squeak
of an ambushed rat
signals where they
pass.

*   *   *

Stars
        are gleaned

by the famished bird
of daybreak

one by one

*   *   *

a hadeda's dawn catarrh
                    lifts
a snot of sound
above the suburbs

* * *

while guineafowl loudly
clatter, panic

as they flee through
a maelstrom of cars

and scatter into
a snapped necklace –

one less lucky
than the others.

* * *

A tern
        white angel
                    unwraps its wings

above the vlei

                is enveloped
by the spray
                    of its dive.

* * *

The hair on the body
of a huntsman stirs in
a sudden morning draft

though it stays
unmoving. Eggs
appended from its
thorax, it's been
chased inside by
the threat of
rain.

     The woman
who eases her back
catching her breath
after washing
the verandah
has not yet
noticed it …

*   *   *

dragonflies lean
sedately on thin limbs
over a rim of birdbath
in delicate parleys
with the noon's fat heat

then a
rumble
of thunder

*   *   *

interlaced with
threads of
soft insistent
drizzle the
praise songs
of frogs
      glisten

* * *

a single caterpillar trying to cross
what must be an

interminable distance from one
side of lawn to the other

stiffening with the effort
                 drowns
                 in a sudden pool
still striving for its goal

* * *

… instead, to be a frog, live
the optimum life:
half land, half water … .

* * *

Is it
a cobra

      insinuated among
   a consternation of
weavers, gleaming

in that tree

a speckled
brown and gold

that vanishes
from sight
among the nests,

deciding when to strike?

*　*　*

Towards dusk one bird lifts its voice
among the matumis and clusterleafs.

– *What species is that,*
flying off?

Listen carefully to its colours,
stare hard at its song:

the bush spreads out
in all directions,

and every branch
now bears its secret.

*   *   *

But a clearing's been made, burgeons in every forest –

in each falls a human shadow.

*   *   *

Fireflies primp, search
for their reflections along
a bracelet of drying pools

*   *   *

always

     the wind

it is

     persuades

trees to

     their shape.

One breath, away

Under a mucilaginous sky
autumn sidles up to us
bearing pandemic.
                    Vuvuzelas
blare, in praise of the humble,
those who watch the tills,
deliver meals, take away
the rubbish of the rich.

A drum taps. Does another?

A wind
          or is that a tickle,
starting in my throat?

In the suburbs, in the slums, on
highways full of tourists' ghosts,
in shacks kinfull of hunger, in
mansions gorging to repletion,
we learn, finally, that death is
an easy menu to order, though
there will be no meal. Our skin:
an edge of calm before the storm.
Our screens,
                    that other comfort food,
reduced to a flicker in the corner.

Late afternoon's an eerie absence:
cars seem to flit past on wheels
of cotton wool, and a silence
masked and not foreseen tiptoes
across the land
             then rumours,
which are enough for fear. What
ever the cards are we're left holding
they're not stacked like plates, with
any care or pattern: so they'll fall
as they may.

Each single day coughs up
food lines
          even as the lungs
of nature start (at last) to reinflate.

Outside the window, at my level,
a sunbird in breeding splendour
eyes me, seems to ask:
"are you then all that's left?"

I can't answer, yet,
             if this landscape
is torn irrevocably, or if its seams
will ever knit us back together:
whether the fog that frays the foot
of nearby hills foretells panic:
                  but
I know that plague is looming,
here.

Nor would the sunbird care:
my species has not been kind to his.

(My God, we'll squeal, "We have
been forsaken!", as if we could
not have seen this coming …).

Concealed owls

1

Time is an owl that broods
on my roof, calling. I breathe
in this night alongside it, beyond
all metaphor, or lore about its
witchery. It's not God's dawn,
(brothers and sisters!) will bring
us to our solace: but how well
we learn to see in the dark.

2

High on a garden pole
he has placed a box
planed to smoothness
as recompense for the
crumbled church spire
and the barn torn down
where cows and donkeys
used to grumble and
stamp themselves to
warmth at night. Owl

does not care. No one
hears its soft passage
before dawn, or sees
those chicks fluff up
into form around
the startlement of
their eyes. Offerings
are gobbled down,

the sweet blood
of the mouse
sacrifice. Living
in what his hands
have made, the only
sign it ever will
reward him with
will be
that final
squeak, cut off.

3

You came up to me, where I mused
in the hide, and said: "Was it you
promised that we'd get to see some owls?

You never showed us the owls!"

4

The poet's an owl: the poem, his pellet.
Among the small bones macerated then expelled,
crushed away from shape, which ones were yours?

Background music

The music here's recycled water
dribbling down a cascade of plastic
rocks. How can 88 keys find no way
in the slightest to discover anything
more disturbing than this key-stuck
whiteness? Black and white, yes,
choose both, not one or the other:
and though our knives and forks
clatter in their turn, can't you find
a counterpoint interesting enough
to let slide these perpetual attempts
to speak in harmony with me?
The piano crammed in its corner
maunders on, but we two stay lost
somewhere in this time and place
where community can only know
itself as klatch. Between fake
marble columns and the maws
of bright, carnivorous windows
around us our people act out their
liberation in innuendo and gossip
with cellphones that burp and blear
fretful as cicadas in the forest
of their need. The promises of
politicians grease the bottom of
each spoon: servility's enacted
here the way it's always been,
except that most of the waitrons
now wear weaves and braids.
Everywhere the question is:
do you buy it? But the answer,
most times, just requires a price.

The actor (a dream of too much light)

1

Expecting as a young man some path of luminosity his footsteps would follow, a passage inevitable as transcribed music

known when heard even for the first time

after four decades on the stage he unearthed just one strand of knowledge: it never would be found. These days – between performances – he hugs himself close in dark room after dark room in motels smelling of mildew, dodging the fiery heart of each stopped noon,

before freeloading off small towns of apathy and smugness.

2

If he opens his curtains towards sunset

he just might find a fly, drunk with the glare, expiring in the window, trapped inside a featureless, unbearable, emphatic chamber of light

no longer abuzz despite the lucid world on the other side of its feet, just beyond its butting head

… a world that for hours has taunted it – so close!…

now it is too late. If it were set free it would no longer seek escape on tattered, unresponsive wings, but blunder into walls at all angles of the compass.

It has become too late to want the world.

Yours hopefully

Dear sir or madam
I come before you as
a humble suppliant
to your poetry magazine.
I have – if I may be
so bold to say – a small
following in my own
country, but I aspire
to greater things which
of course means Europe
or maybe North America
or even anything that
calls itself *Pan-African*.
I am struggling to tame
my poems (such as they
are) into the form you
prefer but alas I'm still
trying. They have peaks
and abysses both in
meaning and in shape
so are just a little bit
jagged unlike your
country which I am
lead to understand by
my cousin Agnes is
pretty flat I must ask
you does this affect
your preferences in
the poetry you publish?
Moreover, very few
clocks in my country

keep proper time so I
have to count on
my fingers over and
over again to find
those meters that
you ask for until
you can say iamb
nonplussed (haha).
I also don't know
any *immigrants* so
I can't really be
ethnic in the way
you want but I am
encouraged by
the fact that you
published a poem
from S up the road
where he talked
about having no
flowers to pick
though you assumed
I think that he was
poor or had no
resources at all like
a watering can
though actually
he and I both live
next to an actual
desert. I think I
should say also
that S's uncle is
our landlord and
my father swears
at him a lot when

he arrives to get
the rent and stare
at my mother but
not of course in
front of him but
sorry what was I
saying? ….

Thorns

Vagabond or visitor
                    the snow
will never drift into my eyes,
won't choke up any pathways,

won't lose traction on my roof,
nor set the skin ashiver. The word
not though, is present always –

here, the noun's the thing vanishes,
melts unashamedly, smears windows ...
snow, not *snow:* the adjective remains.

No change magicking around me: no
silent world to catch, cupped in palm,
awe-filled by its brief existence.

If for once flakes began to fall, for us
who flourish through denial, they'd be
only tiny lepers' bells, a tinkle warily

insistent. Just another wonder to repel.
Like you,
            a dogmatist of drought,
ensnared by the thorns we dwell among,

I've grown old within the parched
landscapes of the heart. So why would
anyone like me – or you, now reading –

find value in a gentleness come suddenly
down upon us all, or seek out its delight?
How on earth do we move on from here?

Imaging

1

And they ask me:
why do you make poems to confuse us?
And I answer: I make poems simply
from those vocables which have fallen out
with their fellows

                        so far as to defend
others than myself against judgment,
against spite, I raise hackles into words

a mirror for reflections
not yet come,
the darkened glimmer
of the psyche,
the chimera of you
I clutch to make desire
more palpable, then
a sudden blazing of release

that lifts its globe-like fingers
in the untrustworthy light of
streetlamps – their shadows –
to knuckle on every door.

2

Spider poems hanging from your ceiling
in that place your broom can't sweep clean,
that only come out at night to eat your flesh
in small, incremental bites –

the envenomed image: stung,
your search desperate for
an antidote finds only
the next word, and the next,
never to be assuaged:

a comma looking for its silence,
a curled snake at the portal
of meaning.

3

The blonde boy whose blue eyes
filled with sorrow until he died
from useless empathy and was transformed,
to become unsightly –

even as a child in a house
under a sky of cages
                              learned
that white was not a colour
until inflected by every other

and another voice still stirs within
that is not ashamed of its skin
nor enclosed by it; but seeks out
the valence of others, their lives
and deaths, for no reason other than
it is the human thing to do.

4

Who are you, to write
as if you knew my life?

How can anyone write the poor?

Whatever the case ...
truth has a middle finger,

lifts it often.

5

Long ago
I made the trip from thirst-stricken life to water.
My feet are muddy.

But if you walk towards the river,
I will walk away.

Aubade

Why is it impossible to save a dawn?
Today, for instance, began improbably.
Streaking lightened the ebony around Venus
as it sagged towards the skyline, then
a green lid slowly prised open to reveal
a yawning mouth of jagged mountains
coming slowly out of sleep.
                                         All night
I had stared up, feverless, as forms
of shadow built then broke themselves
abstractedly across the ceiling
                                         but now
wisps of cirrus sliced through by contrails
flare orange as the sun uplifts, while to
its god of warmth a fluffed starling wheedles
thin praise, invoking resurrection. Smog
dissipates like smoke up from the shacklands
and the breaths of the homeless under bridges
coalesce above their blankets. The sun pinks
out trucks already high up a hill of garbage,
tipping

          tipping my hat to it all, who am I,
head stuck inside a jersey, ready to take leave?

Nature litigates against the body in unlikely ways,
always renewing the apprehension of old men
as they listen to the blood pound at their temples
and arthritis speak its discomfort ever louder
in their bones. The sun, now brash, flints
against roofs, trash cans, draws our cells out
towards a final dance. What awaits me,
irritated these days even by that single starling
stupidly trying to hammer *"my home, my home"*
into these wooden eaves? I need to scurry out
before the coming heat: lock the door, watch
out for cars, pick up the pace! I know

dawn is inexhaustible. My dawns are not.

Postlude

As of now my neighbours
have discovered joy

the patriarch must be asleep
for his daughters giggle
at a joke so new
it smirks at ancient homilies
behind the windows
there is a constant plaint
of pacing sandals
and doeks in motion
more candles spark to life
in every room and tremble
while outside
                    between us
under the fall and rustle
of a gigantic moulting tree
the skulduggery of stray cats
with hallucinatory eyes
hunting moths and geckoes
for once proves fruitless

no blood will be spilled tonight

and sorrow is no longer
enraptured with my face.

Acknowledgments:

Gennady Aygi *Into the Snow: Selected Poems* (Seattle & New York: Wave Books, 2011); John Berryman *Dream Songs* (London: Faber, 1990); Vahni Capildeo *Measures of Expatriation* (Manchester: Carcanet, 2016); Phillippa Yaa de Villiers *ice cream headache in my bone* (Cape Town: Modjaji, 2017); Frantz Fanon *The Wretched of the Earth* (London: Penguin, 1967); Paavo Haavikko *Selected Poems* (Manchester: Carcanet, 1991); Ada Limón *Sharks in the Rivers* (Minneapolis: Milkweed, 2010); Douglas Oliver *Islands of Voices: Selected Poems* (Swindon: Shearsman, 2020); Giuseppe Ungaretti *Selected Poems* (New York: FSG, 2002).
'Kind' and 'Birding' converse with poems by Douglas Oliver ('For Kind') and Paavo Haavikko ('The Winter Palace: Second Poem') respectively. 'Prelude' begins with a line from Giuseppe Ungaretti's 'Resting.' 'People in glass houses' was prompted by listening to Kate Kilalea discuss Bruno Tait's proposed Alpine City.

Thanks are due to many people, especially Stephen Clingman, Colleen Crawford Cousins, Colleen Higgs, Rochelle Kapp, Rustum Kozain and Stephen Symons.

Printed in the United States
by Baker & Taylor Publisher Services